NOV - - 2014

THE CHANGING CLIMATE OF
AFRICA

Patricia K. Kummer

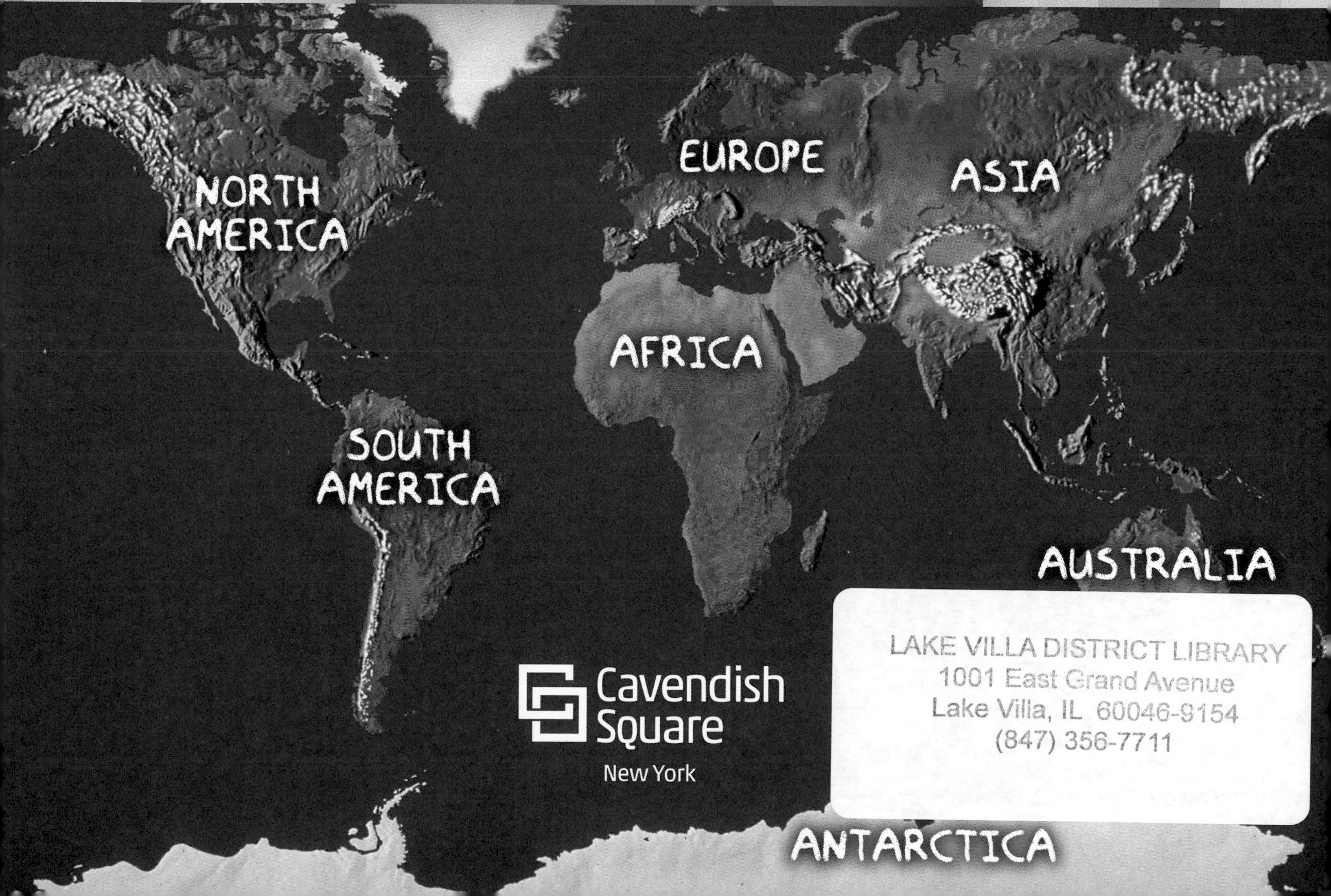

NORTH AMERICA

SOUTH AMERICA

EUROPE

ASIA

AFRICA

AUSTRALIA

ANTARCTICA

Cavendish Square

New York

Published in 2014 by Cavendish Square Publishing, LLC
303 Park Avenue South, Suite 1247, New York, NY 10010

Library of Congress Cataloging-in-Publication Data
Kummer, Patricia K.
The changing climate of Africa / by Patricia K. Kummer.
p. cm. — (Climates and continents)
Includes index.
ISBN 978-1-62712-437-9 (hardcover) ISBN 978-1-62712-438-6 (paperback) ISBN 978-1-62712-439-3 (ebook)
1. Climatic changes — Environmental aspects — Africa. 2. Climatic changes — Effect of human beings on — Africa. I. Kummer, Patricia K.
II. Title.
QC903.2.A35 K86 2014
577.22—dc23

Editorial Director: Dean Miller
Senior Editor: Peter Mavrikis
Copy Editor: Cynthia Roby
Art Director: Jeffrey Talbot
Designer: Amy Greenan
Photo Researcher: Alison Morretta
Production Manager: Jennifer Ryder-Talbot
Production Editor: Andrew Coddington

Expert Reader: Victor Savage, associate professor, Department of Geography, National University of Singapore

The photographs in this book are used by permission and through the courtesy of: Cover photo by Peeter Viisimaa/Vetta/Getty Images, Davor Pukljak/Shutterstock.com; Davor Pukljak/Shutterstock.com, 4; Mapping Specialists, 6; Brian D Cruickshank/Lonely Planet Images/Getty Images, 8; Daryl Balfour/Gallo Images/Getty Images, 11; Herman Emmet/Photo Researchers/Getty Images, 12; Mapping Specialists, 13; John Warburton-Lee/AWL Images/Getty Images, 14; Chris Johns/Contributor/National Geographic/Getty Images, 15; Lonely Planet/Lonely Planet Images/Getty Images, 17; joSon/The Image Bank/Getty Images, 18; Max Alexander/Dorling Kindersley/Getty Images, 19; Christian Aslund/Lonely Planet Images/Getty Images, 21; Eco Images/Universal Images Group/Getty Images, 22; Everett Collection / SuperStock, 23; Mint Images - Frans Lanting/Mint Images/Getty Images, 24; Per-Gunnar Ostby/Oxford Scientific/Getty Images, 27; Mint Images - Frans Lanting/Mint Images/Getty Images, 28; Ignacio Palacios/Lonely Planet Images/Getty Images, 29; NHPA / SuperStock, 33; Eric L. Wheater/Lonely Planet Images/Getty Images, 34; Jane Sweeney/Lonely Planet Images/Getty Images, 34; Ruth Eastham & Max Paoli/Lonely Planet Images/Getty Images, 35; Mary Cochran/Flickr Open/Getty Images, 36; Nigel Pavitt/AWL Images/Getty Images, 39; age fotostock / SuperStock, 40; Heinrich van den Berg/Gallo Images/Getty Images, 41.

Printed in the United States of America

CONTENTS

ONE The Oldest Continent 5

TWO An Extreme Landscape 11

THREE Warming Temperatures, Varying Rainfall 20

FOUR A Changing Natural Environment. 26

FIVE People and Change 32

SIX Looking for Solutions
to Present-day Problems. 37

Glossary. 42

Find Out More. 44

Index. 46

ONE

THE OLDEST CONTINENT

ooking at a globe or at a world map, it is quite easy to identify the seven **continents**. They are Earth's largest pieces of land. As you can see from the map on page 6, Africa is the second-largest continent. Only Asia is larger. The other five continents in order of size are North America, South America, Antarctica, Europe, and Australia.

Getting To Know Africa

Africa covers about 23 percent of Earth's land. This large continent is completely surrounded by water and includes several islands. To the west, Africa is bordered by the Atlantic Ocean. To the north, the Mediterranean Sea separates Africa from Europe. To the east, the Suez Canal and Red Sea separate Africa from Asia. The Indian Ocean forms

This photo taken from a satellite in space captures Africa's huge size—the second-largest of the seven continents.

POLITICAL MAP OF AFRICA

Where in the World Is Africa?

Use the political map on page 6 to answer the following questions about the continent of Africa:

1. Which country has land in both Africa and Asia?

2. Which region is closest to Europe?

3. Which region is bordered by the Red Sea, Gulf of Aden, and Indian Ocean?

4. Which region is bordered by the Indian Ocean and the Atlantic Ocean?

5. Which region has the smallest coastline?

6. Which region has three countries with no coastline? What are those countries?

On the map, the solid line is the Equator. The top dotted line is the Tropic of Cancer. The bottom dotted line is the Tropic of Capricorn.

the rest of Africa's eastern border. At Africa's southern tip, the waters of the Atlantic and Indian oceans mix together.

Africa's landmass is often divided into five regions—North, East, Central, West, and Southern Africa. The land, climate, or people in each of Africa's five regions have some features in common. For example, East Africa has most of the continent's highest land.

Most of Africa lies in the tropics—between the Tropic of Cancer and the Tropic of Capricorn. This location gives Africa mainly hot and wet, and hot and dry climates. Africa's climates and landforms provide **habitats** for some of the world's most amazing plants and animals.

Africa also has the world's fastest-growing population. Africa's people belong to more than 3,000 ethnic groups. Each group shares the same language and culture and lives in a special area. The Arabs and Berbers in North Africa, the Bambuti Pygmy and Fang in Central Africa, and the San and Afrikaners in Southern Africa are some of Africa's ethnic groups.

The Continents and Change

For hundreds of millions of years, Africa and the other continents have undergone slow, continuous change. In fact about 250 million years ago, there was only one continent—Pangaea. The continent that became known as Africa was toward the center of Pangaea. Gradually, Pangaea broke apart. The other six continents drifted thousands of miles north, south, east, or west. Africa shifted only slightly to the northeast. It has been in its final location longer than the other continents. That is why Africa is the oldest continent.

Change continues to happen to Earth and its continents today. Earth's crust is made up of many **tectonic plates**. These hard, rigid sheets of solid rock are always moving. Most of the time, they slide past one another. Sometimes they crash into each other, slip over or under each other, or pull apart. Those movements result in earthquakes, volcanic eruptions, mountain building, and **rifting**. Africa has experienced all of those events.

Climate change is also affecting Africa, as well as the other continents. It is caused in part by how people use the land and its resources. Africa's quickly growing population has changed the land in many ways. Some of those changes have harmed the natural environment. In recent years, people and countries in Africa started working to improve the environment. Some projects are beginning to show good results.

Africa's Highs and Lows

East Africa has the continent's highest and lowest points—Mount Kilimanjaro in Tanzania and Lake Assal in Djibouti. The mountain and lake are far apart, but volcanic eruptions created both. Kilimanjaro is a dormant (sleeping) volcano that still rumbles. At 19,340 feet (5,895 meters) above sea level, Kilimanjaro is the world's tallest mountain that is not part of a mountain range. It is popular with mountain climbers. As they go up, climbers pass through rainforest, flowery meadows, and a desert-like area before reaching the snowy, glacier-covered summit.

Far to the northeast, Lake Assal developed in the crater of a volcano. This salty lake is 509 feet (155 m) below sea level. Lake Assal does not attract swimmers or fishers, though. Instead, miners come in camel caravans. They remove salt from the 203-foot- (62-m-) deep field that encircles the lake. High temperatures cause the lake's water to evaporate, leaving behind the world's largest salt reserve.

TWO

AN EXTREME LANDSCAPE

African elephants cross the open plains of Amboseli National Park in Kenya. Mount Kibo is in the background.

Africa's landscape has some of the world's best-known features, such as the Nile River and the Sahara Desert. Africa's most unusual feature, though, is the Great Rift Valley. This great tear in the earth happened between 30 and 66 million years ago. Tectonic plate movement and heat escaping from underground volcanoes caused the earth to drop.

11

The Great Rift Valley in Africa stretches from Ethiopia to Mozambique.

The Great Rift Valley is the world's longest, widest, and deepest crack. Rifting continues to happen in this part of Africa. In 2005 in Ethiopia, a 35-mile- (56-kilometer-) long, 20-foot- (6- m-) wide crack opened in just five days. Since then, other long cracks have occurred in Uganda and Malawi. Scientists think that rifting will pull eastern Africa away from the rest of the continent.

A Continent on a Plateau

Africa's elevation is also unusual. Overall, Africa is about 1,300 feet (396 m) higher above sea level than the other continents. The same movements that formed the Great Rift Valley also pushed all of Africa upward. That action made Africa mainly a plateau. Based on the height of the plateau, Africa is divided into two regions—High Africa and Low Africa.

High Africa includes the Ethiopian, East African, and Southern plateaus. The land there averages more than 3,000 feet (914 m) above sea level. Some of these highlands have grassy areas with fertile soil.

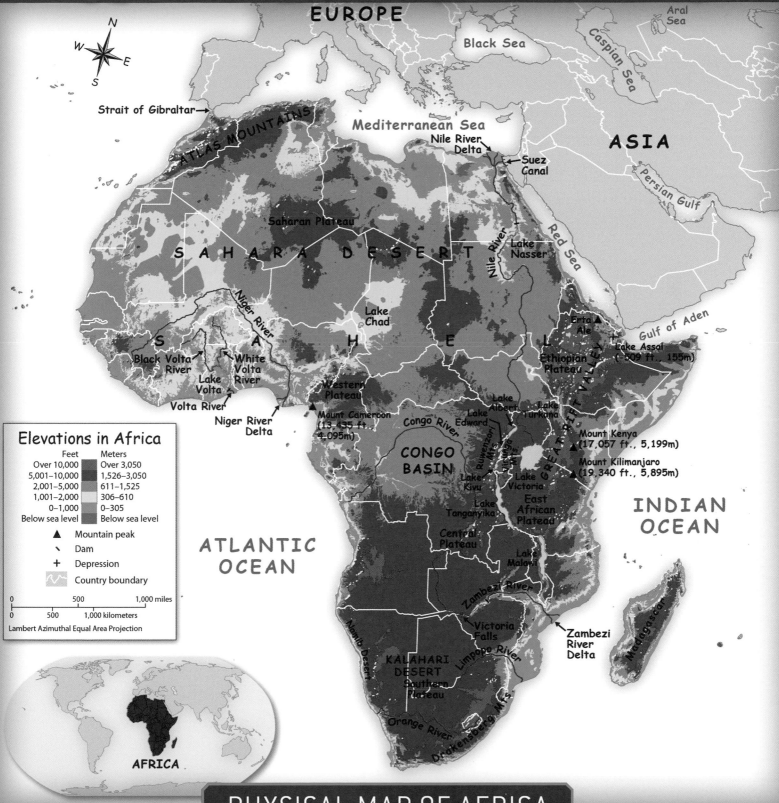

PHYSICAL MAP OF AFRICA

EUROPE

Black Sea

Aral Sea

Caspian Sea

Strait of Gibraltar →

ATLAS MOUNTAINS

Mediterranean Sea

Nile River Delta

ASIA

Suez Canal

Persian Gulf

Saharan Plateau

S A H A R A   D E S E R T

Nile River

Lake Nasser

Red Sea

Niger River

Lake Chad

S A H E L

Erta Ale ▲

Gulf of Aden

Black Volta River

White Volta River

Lake Volta

Volta River

Ethiopian Plateau

Lake Assal (−509 ft., 155m) +

Western Plateau

Mount Cameroon (13,435 ft., 4,095m) ▲

Niger River Delta

Congo River

Lake Albert

Lake Edward

Lake Turkana

Mount Kenya (17,057 ft., 5,199m) ▲

CONGO BASIN

Ruwenzori Mts.

Virunga Mts.

Mount Kilimanjaro (19,340 ft., 5,895m) ▲

Lake Kivu

Lake Victoria

GREAT RIFT VALLEY

INDIAN OCEAN

Lake Tanganyika

East African Plateau

ATLANTIC OCEAN

Central Plateau

Lake Malawi

Madagascar

Namib Desert

Zambezi River

Victoria Falls

Zambezi River Delta

Limpopo River

KALAHARI DESERT

Southern Plateau

Orange River

Drakensberg Mts.

Elevations in Africa

Feet	Meters
Over 10,000	Over 3,050
5,001–10,000	1,526–3,050
2,001–5,000	611–1,525
1,001–2,000	306–610
0–1,000	0–305
Below sea level	Below sea level

▲ Mountain peak
↘ Dam
+ Depression
〜 Country boundary

0   500   1,000 miles
0   500   1,000 kilometers
Lambert Azimuthal Equal Area Projection

AFRICA

Others have rich volcanic soil. All of these soils provide land that is good for growing crops and for grazing livestock. Under the Southern Plateau lie the world's richest deposits of diamonds and gold.

The Sahara, Western, and Central plateaus make up most of Low Africa. The land there is only 500 to 2,000 feet (150–610 m) above sea level. The Sahara Desert and rainforest cover most of Low Africa's plateaus.

Shaded by an acacia tree in Kenya, a Maasai warrior walks in the direction of Mount Kenya.

From Mountains to Plains

Africa has few mountain ranges. Many of their peaks have been worn down by wind and rain. The Atlas Mountains in North Africa are the continent's longest range. Berber people have carved terraces in those mountains for growing grains, fruits, and vegetables. In Central Africa, the Ruwenzori and Virunga ranges rise just west of the Great Rift Valley. Volcanoes formed the Virunga Range, as well as the Drakensberg Range near Southern Africa's eastern coast. Single mountains, such as Mounts Cameroon, Kenya, and Kilimanjaro were also formed by volcanoes.

In 1978, the earth split apart in this volcanic area along Djibouti's coast. Each year, the crack widens. With continued rifting, this land could be underwater someday.

Most of Africa's plains are located in a narrow strip along its northwestern, northern, and eastern coasts. These coastal plains include desert, swampland, and fertile farmland for growing fruits, nuts, and sugarcane. Africa's largest inland plain is the Serengeti Plain on the floor of the Great Rift Valley. The plain's vast grasslands provide grazing land for large herds of wild animals and for cattle.

Vast Deserts

About 40 percent of Africa is desert. The Sahara Desert—the world's largest—covers most of North Africa. Swirling sand dunes make up only 25 percent of the Sahara. The rest is bare rock and gravel. Oases with watering holes, date palms, and sparse grasses break up the harsh environment. Herders graze their camels, goats, and sheep on the grasses. Some oases support crops of olives, figs, citrus fruit, and barley. Beneath the Sahara lie large deposits of oil, natural gas, and phosphate.

Getting the Lay of the Land

MAPPING SKILLS

Study the physical map of Africa on page 13 to answer the following questions:

1. Which of Africa's plateaus has the highest land?

2. Which of Africa's deserts has the largest amount of low lands?

3. Which desert is on the highest land?

4. Where is the source of the Nile River?

5. What lake was formed by dams on the Volta River?

6. Which mountain peak is on Africa's coast?

ANSWERS:
1. Ethiopian Plateau
2. Sahara
3. Kalahari
4. Lake Victoria
5. Lake Volta
6. Mount Cameroon

Africa's other deserts are in Southern Africa. The Namib Desert's pink-to-orange sands line the continent's southwestern coast. Tungsten is mined below the desert, and salt is taken from the surface. The

The Namib Desert is famous for colorful sand dunes, such as these in Namibia's Namib-Naukluft National Park.

southeastern edge of the Namib connects with the Kalahari Desert. Under the Kalahari lie large deposits of coal, copper, and nickel. The world's largest diamond mine, an **open-pit mine**, is in Botswana's part of the desert.

Rivers, Lakes, and Coastline

At 4,160 miles (6,695 km) long, the Nile River is the world's longest one. Some of Africa's best farmland is in the Nile Valley and on the Nile Delta. Other rivers also formed deltas where they empty into the ocean. The Zambezi Delta also has rich farmland. The Niger Delta has large oil deposits. Africa's rivers have many waterfalls and rapids. To control those rivers, dams have been built. Some dams have hydroelectric

Victoria Falls

Victoria Falls is one of the seven natural wonders of the world. The British explorer David Livingstone named the falls for Queen Victoria in 1855. Local people still call it Mosi-oa-Tunya (the Smoke that Thunders), though. Victoria Falls is located on the Zambezi River between Zambia and Zimbabwe. At the falls, the Zambezi flows over a 1.25-mile- (2-km-) wide basalt cliff and crashes down 360 feet (108 m).

This is known as the world's largest sheet of falling water. From miles away, the falls' spray can be seen and its roar can be heard. On nights with full moons, "moon bows" can be seen through the mist.

The Aswan High Dam, built across the Nile River in Egypt, was completed in 1970.

power plants. They generate electricity for Africa's cities. The dams also help prevent flooding by holding large amounts of water in **reservoirs**.

Africa has more than 600 lakes, including reservoirs. The largest ones are East Africa's Great Lakes. Lake Victoria is the continent's largest, and the world's second-largest, freshwater lake. Lakes Albert, Edward, Kivu, Malawi, Tanganyika, and Turkana are long, narrow lakes. They formed at the bottom of the Great Rift Valley. Lake Tanganyika is the world's longest freshwater lake. In West Africa, Lake Chad was once Africa's fourth-largest lake. Since 1960, it has lost 95 percent of its size. Years with little rainfall along with farmers using the lake to irrigate their fields led to this disaster. As the lake shrinks, **desertification** occurs. This allows the Sahara Desert to expand south. Desertification causes even less rain to fall.

Africa has a short coastline because there are only a few bays, harbors, and gulfs. Parts of the coast have experienced changes. Saltwater has overflowed the Nile and Zambezi deltas and damaged good farmland. A rise in the Indian Ocean's tides has eroded beaches and seawalls along the eastern coast. People have had to leave their homes and towns.

19

THREE

WARMING TEMPERATURES, VARYING RAINFALL

Because the Equator runs across the center of Africa, half of the continent experiences winter while it is summer in the other half. Most of Africa has year-round hot, or at least warm, weather, though. That is because Africa has more land in the tropics than any other continent. Still, Africa's highlands and mountain areas can get quite cold. North Africa has experienced the continent's most extreme temperatures. At 136 degrees Fahrenheit (58 degrees Celsius), the world's highest temperature, recorded September 13, 1922, was in the desert at Al Aziziyah, Libya. Africa's lowest temperature, recorded February 11, 1935, was -11°F (-24°C) in Ifrane, Morocco, in the Atlas Mountains.

Varying amounts of rainfall, not temperature, are what make Africa's climate zones so different from one another. In the wet tropical rainforest, Mount Cameroon receives Africa's largest amount of annual

The snow-covered mountains of the Atlas Range stretch across northern Africa from Morocco to Tunisia.

rainfall—about 405 inches (1,029 cm). Africa's least amount of annual rain falls in northern Sudan's arid (dry) desert—less than 0.1 inches (0.25 cm). Between those two climates are the wet/dry tropics with one or two yearly rainy seasons. That's where Africa's grassy **savannas** are located.

Climate Change in Africa

Major differences in temperatures and precipitation over several years are known as climate change. Some of Africa's climate change is caused from **magma** that heats the ground as it pushes up toward Earth's surface. Africa's people have also caused climate change. As the population increased, some people moved into areas where no one had lived before. To develop farms, they cut down large areas of the tropical rainforest. They also turned grassy savannas into cropland. Changes made to forests and grasslands affect the climate. Temperatures increase and rainfall decreases.

21

In Sudan, herders draw water for their goats. Overgrazing of herds has led to desertification and has contributed to land erosion.

Other people moved to Africa's cities. Some of their homes, apartments, and offices have air conditioning that requires **chlorofluorocarbons**. Many people in both rural and urban Africa use wood or charcoal for cooking. They need gasoline to power cars, motorbikes, busses, and trucks. All of those coolants and fuels give off gases that contribute to more climate change and also cause air pollution.

Results of Climate Change

During the past 100 years, Africa has experienced climate change. Temperatures have become warmer by about 0.9°F (0.5°C). That is slightly less than the world's average increase of 1.3°F (0.74°C). The amount of rainfall over Africa has changed, too. In parts of East and Southern Africa, heavier rains have caused floods that have damaged farm fields and towns. In dry lands such as the Sahel even less rain has fallen. That has led to years of **drought** and **famine**.

Throughout Africa, the warming climate has affected the environment. Since 1912, most of the glaciers on Mount Kenya, on Mount Kilimanjaro, and in the Ruwenzori Mountains have disappeared. Scientists forecast that most of Africa's glaciers will be gone by 2020. Rivers that once received water from melting glaciers are now going dry. Africa is losing an important source of fresh water.

Another effect of climate change is the warming of ocean waters. As the oceans become warmer, their water expands. This in turn causes sea levels to rise. Higher sea levels have already occurred on the Atlantic Coast in Senegal, along the Mediterranean Sea in Egypt, and in places along the Indian Ocean. Warmer oceans have also caused less rainfall in the Sahel and in drier areas of East and Southern Africa.

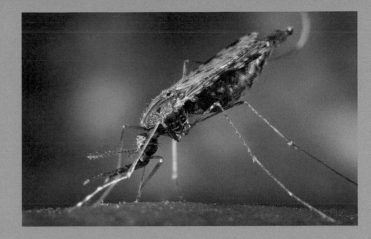

Climate-related Health Problem: Malaria

Climate change in Africa is allowing diseases such as malaria to spread. Malaria is caused by the bite from an Anopheles mosquito. These mosquitoes thrive in Africa's warm, wet weather. Because of climate change, Anopheles mosquitoes have moved to higher altitudes, which have become warmer. Now, people in Africa's mountains and highlands suffer from malaria's fevers, chills, and headaches.

Tai National Park

Tai National Park covers 1,274 square miles (330,000 ha) in southwestern Côte d'Ivoire's rainforest. Rain still falls year-round in the southern part of the park. Climate change caused by cutting down nearby rainforests has brought a dry season to the northern park. During the dry months, winds called harmattans bring dust from the Sahara to the park's northern forest.

Tai National Park is important because it contains the last area of West Africa's primary (never cut) rainforest. Some of its trees are more than 150

feet (46 m) tall. Other trees have stilt-like roots that reach into rivers for water. An important rainforest tree is the Terminalia superba. Commonly known as "the tree of malaria," its bark is used by local people for the treatment of that disease. Altogether, Tai National Park has about 1,300 kinds of trees and other plants.

Hundreds of different kinds of animals live there too, including African forest elephants, buffaloes, giant forest hogs, anteaters, and several kinds of monkeys. Animals on the **endangered species** list are the park's pygmy hippopotamus, Olive colobus monkey, two kinds of forest duikers (small antelopes), and West African chimpanzee. The chimpanzees are known for working together using stone tools to crack open wild nuts.

Natural Disasters

Africa's natural disasters are caused by earthquakes, volcanoes, and **cyclones**. In eastern Africa, more magma is pushing toward Earth's surface, causing frequent earthquakes and volcanoes. In recent years, strong quakes have occurred from Djibouti to Malawi. They have destroyed buildings in towns and villages. After one quake, the ground in Malawi was about 20 inches (50 cm) higher.

Africa has nine active volcanoes. Most of them are in Central and East Africa. The most recent eruption occurred in 2011 at Erta Ale in Ethiopia. Lava from eruptions destroys nearby property. But it also enriches the soil. Some of Africa's most valuable crops, such as coffee, tea, and bananas, grow in volcanic soil.

Cyclones frequently strike Mozambique, South Africa, and Madagascar. Those severe windstorms start in the Indian Ocean near the Equator. In those areas, warm, wet air rises and starts spinning. When cyclones hit Southern Africa, their winds of up to 200 miles (322 km) per hour cause much damage. Heavy rains from the storms cause severe flooding far inland. Cyclones have damaged Africa's southeastern coast and brought seawater onto farmlands.

A CHANGING NATURAL ENVIRONMENT

Nature and people have made many changes to Africa's land and bodies of water. In turn those changes have affected the habitats of the continent's plants and animals.

A Shrinking Rainforest

About 20 percent of Africa is covered with rainforest. Most of that land is in West Africa, Central Africa's Congo Basin, and Madagascar. Unfortunately, **deforestation** has damaged large parts of Africa's rainforest. Local people chopped down trees and used the wood to build small houses and for firewood for cooking. Logging companies cut large areas of ebony and mahogany trees. Their wood is used to make furniture, cabinets, flooring, and trim for houses throughout the world.

Some of Africa's remaining original rainforest stands on Mount Cameroon in Cameroon. The rainforest continues to disappear because Africans rely on wood as a source for cooking and heating.

With the trees gone, farmers burned the remaining plants—orchids, ferns, mosses, and vines. They turned those parts of the rainforest into farmland. There they grow crops to feed their families. Large companies built coffee, cacao (cocoa), and palm oil tree **plantations** on other rainforest land. Those crops are sold to people in other parts of the world.

Deforestation has caused many animals to lose their rainforest homes. The Congo peacock, dwarf chimpanzee, African slender-snouted crocodile, leopard, and small forest elephant are a few endangered rainforest animals. Overhunting has endangered other animals, such as monkeys, gorillas, and chimpanzees. Local people eat their meat or sell it to restaurants. Deforestation has also caused many years of drought in parts of the Sahel.

One-of-a-Kind Madagascar

Madagascar, located east of Mozambique, is the world's fourth-largest island. This land pulled away from the continent of Africa about 165 million years ago. Far from other land for so long, many unusual plants and animals developed on Madagascar. Octopus trees (as shown below) grow in the western Spiny Desert. The Avenue of the Baobabs is a group of trees that border a road in western Madagascar. Scientists think baobab trees started in Madagascar. The eastern side of Madagascar is rainforest. The vanilla orchid grows

there. Much of the rainforest has been cut down and turned into farmland. Still, more than seventy kinds of lemurs live there. The indri lemur makes a sound like a police siren. The world's largest and smallest chameleons also live in Madagascar's rainforest.

In the annual migration, wildebeests and zebras travel together across the open savanna.

A Changing Savanna

About 40 percent of Africa is covered with savanna. Short and tall grasses, small groupings of thorn bushes, and flat-topped acacia and broad-trunked baobab trees grow on the savanna. All those plants can withstand fires and drought.

Some of Africa's best-known animals live on the savanna. They include the world's largest, tallest, and fastest land animals—the bush elephant, the giraffe, and the cheetah. Every year, about a million wildebeests along with huge herds of zebras and gazelles migrate north over the Serengeti Plain to Maasai Mara and back again. They follow the rains and then graze on the fresh grasses. Some of those migrating animals are caught by the savanna's lions, cheetahs, hyenas, and wild dogs. Because parts of the savanna are receiving less rain, many animals are losing their food supply and becoming endangered.

More people are also moving onto savanna lands. Local farmers are planting crops. Maasai people graze their cattle on the Serengeti. In other places, herders let their livestock graze too long in one spot. Those activities have caused parts of the savanna to lose its grasses. Desertification takes place when the grasses disappear. If the savanna is near a desert, sands move onto the now-bare grassland.

Expanding Deserts

About 40 percent of Africa is already covered by deserts. Climate change and overgrazing of savannas and the Sahel cause the deserts to continue to expand. The Sahara spreads both north and south a few miles every year. The Kalahari has stretched onto land that was overgrazed by flocks of sheep.

The deserts themselves support few plants and animals. Most desert plants need long roots to seek water far underground. The Welwitschia plant, which grows only in the Namib Desert, has short roots, though. It absorbs water from the fog that rolls over the Namib from the Atlantic Ocean. Some of these plants are 2,000 years old. The Welwitschia has become endangered because people collect it to pick and sell its seeds.

Desert animals also have special ways to exist in the harsh environment. During the heat of the day, scorpions stay under the sand and hedgehogs remain in their burrows. The large ears of fennec foxes allow heat to escape from their bodies. Desert antelopes and gazelles can go for long periods of time without water. Both of those Saharan animals are now endangered because of overhunting.

Changes along Rivers, Lakes, and Coastlines

Some of Africa's rivers are drying up because of climate change. Others are losing water because dams, irrigation for farming, and refuse from mining have changed the rivers' flow. This limits the habitat for the hippopotamus and crocodile.

Lake Victoria has lost almost 200 kinds of fish because the Nile perch and Nile tilapia were placed in the lake. Those large fish ate most of the smaller native fish. Small cichlid could be air-dried before they were eaten. Because the new fish are oily, they must be smoked. That requires large amounts of firewood, leading to pollution and deforestation.

Africa's east and west coastlines have suffered from other problems. Oil spills have damaged the Niger Delta, harming the habitat of waterbirds and fish. Along Ghana's coast, mangrove forests have been cut down. The roots of those trees served as breeding places for fish, shrimp, and crabs. On East Africa's coast, fishing trawlers are destroying seagrass beds. Dugong, known as sea cows, feed on them.

Menacing Water Plants

Along the Nile, Niger, and Zambezi rivers, barriers of sudd have developed. Those clumps of papyrus, reeds, and floating Nile cabbage harm fishing and block the rivers for boats. In many areas, sudd accumulated because dams slowed the flow of a river's water.

Another problem plant is the water hyacinth. It was imported as a special pond plant, but it spread to rivers and lakes. This plant can cover an entire body of water, killing the fish.

FIVE

PEOPLE AND CHANGE

In addition to being the oldest continent, Africa is also known as the birthplace of the human race. Descendants of those early people left Africa and gradually populated the other continents. Currently, more than 1 billion people live in Africa—about 15 percent of the world's people. Only Asia has a larger population. Africa's largest country is Nigeria with about 166 million people. Seychelles, an island country in the Indian Ocean, has Africa's smallest population—about 90,000 people.

Changes in Population Growth

Africa has the world's fastest-growing population. Each year, it increases by about 26 million people. The reason for this growth is that Africa has the world's youngest population. About 49 percent of the population is under 18 years of age. As those children grow up, they will have their

The Maasai, such as these men in Tanzania's Serengeti National Park, are semi-nomadic people.

own children. By 2050, about 1.8 billion people will be living in Africa. Then, Africa will have about 20 percent of the world's people. In some African countries, such as Uganda, Nigeria, and Ethiopia, the population will double or triple in size.

Leaders throughout Africa are working to slow this growth by encouraging people to have smaller families. They know that Africa's land cannot feed so many people. Africans already suffer from food and water shortages. About 28 percent of African children under 5 years of age are underweight. They do not get enough to eat. By 2050, the population of Lesotho is estimated to decrease. The populations in Tunisia, Botswana, Swaziland, and South Africa are estimated to have only small increases. In those countries, the level of education has risen and the birthrate has decreased.

Where Africa's People Live

Africa's most heavily populated area is the Nile River Valley in Egypt. In fact, that is the world's most heavily populated area. Other highly populated areas are along the north and southeast coasts, the highlands

Endangered People

Besides endangered plants and animals, some of Africa's people and languages are endangered, too. At least 6 million Africans are refugees. They fled from their own countries and found protection in other African countries. Many people of the Sahel became refugees because of food shortages caused by long droughts. Other refugees are members of ethnic groups that were being killed in local wars. When people move into new areas, their lives change. Sometimes they must learn a new language. About 50 of Africa's 1,000 languages are already extinct. Another 50 are endangered as fewer people now speak them.

A Pokot girl from Kenya wears traditional beads (above). A Karo man in Ethiopia is covered with symbolic body paint (below).

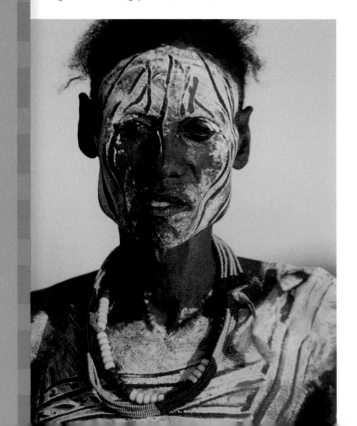

This semi-nomadic Berber man in North Africa wears a traditional robe and headgear, which protect him from the Sahara Desert's heat and sand.

of Ethiopia, the Great Lakes, and the Niger Delta. Africa's best farmland and largest cities are in those places.

Africa also has the world's largest rural population—about 60 percent. In some countries that number is even higher. For example, more than 80 percent of the people in Ethiopia, Malawi, Niger, Rwanda, Swaziland, and Uganda live in rural areas. Most rural people live in farming villages. Others, such as the Dinka, Fulani, Maasai, and Zulu, move across the savanna or from oasis to oasis on the desert. Those herders find grazing land for their livestock. Bambuti Pygmies—people who are less than 5 feet (1.5 m) tall—live in the rainforest where they hunt and gather roots, berries, and nuts. Still other rural people fish in Africa's lakes and along the coastline.

The other 40 percent of Africa's people live in or near urban areas—large cities. Of course, some countries have a larger percentage of city dwellers. All the countries in North Africa except Egypt are more than 58 percent urban. Even more people live in the cities of Djibouti (76 percent), Gabon (86 percent), and South Africa (62 percent). Africans will continue to move to urban areas. Making a living from farming, herding, and fishing is becoming harder. Africa's cities can offer jobs in nearby oil, gold, and diamond mining industries. By 2030, about 55 percent of Africans will be living in cities.

Cairo, Egypt – Africa's Largest City

Cairo is Egypt's capital and Africa's largest city with a population of almost 11 million people. In CE 989, the city was founded on the banks of the Nile River in northern Egypt's desert. Today, Cairo has spread west to the Sphinx and the ancient pyramids at Giza.

The city is known for blending ancient and modern ways of life. Cars and trucks travel through the city on expressways. The subway moves people underground. Tall glass-and-steel office buildings and hotels stand along the Nile. Not far from the river is the Egyptian Antiquities Museum. There, the mummies of Egyptian pharaohs (kings) are on view. A few blocks away, people walk down narrow streets. They shop at bazaars (outdoor marketplaces) that offer everything from handmade rugs and leather goods to camels.

SIX
LOOKING FOR SOLUTIONS TO PRESENT-DAY PROBLEMS

Africa's fast-growing population is running out of usable, livable land. People have overused much of Africa's farmland. They have damaged parts of the rainforest and savanna. Those actions plus the activities of people in other parts of the world have caused climate change in Africa. Africa's leaders and people are trying to correct these problems.

Africa's Major Problems

Africa's main problem is its rapidly growing population. Most Africans live in rural areas, but the land cannot support them. In the past ten years, several million Africans have died from starvation. Many of them were children. More Africans continue to move to cities. But Africa's cities are already having problems with shortages of electricity and clean water. In addition, more than half of Africa's urban residents live in slums. Their homes are built with scraps of wood and tin. Most have dirt floors and no windows. In slum areas, there is little or no electricity and no indoor plumbing.

Another problem is education. Many parents cannot afford to send their children to school. In addition, some countries cannot afford to build many schools or to pay teachers. Only about 75 percent of Africa's children attend elementary school. Less than 40 percent attend high school. Some students stop going to school after fifth grade. In Africa, girls often do not go to school because they must help with work at home. With a poor education system, Africa is not gaining the smart leaders and workers that it needs.

Health care is another major problem. Many African countries cannot afford to build enough hospitals and clinics. Africa also has fewer doctors and nurses than other parts of the world. Because of the climate, Africans suffer from many tropical diseases. Malaria kills about one million Africans each year. Sleeping sickness, which is caused from tsetse fly bites, also kills or weakens many Africans. In addition, the lack of clean water for drinking and cooking leads to other diseases. Because of these health problems, Africans, on average, live to be only 52 years of age. About 8 percent of Africa's children do not reach their first birthday.

Still another problem is climate change. As Africa's temperatures continue to increase and rainfalls decrease, more land will become desert. As glaciers melt and rivers dry up, supplies of fresh, clean water will decrease. As saltwater floods more fertile farmland, food crops will be in even shorter supply. And people will have to find new homes farther inland. Desertification and flooding also hurt Africa's plants and animals. By 2085, as much as 40 percent of Africa's plant and animal species will have lost their habitats. Then, Africa's animals and people will compete even harder for food, water, and land.

People fish from boats on Uganda's side of Lake Victoria, a major source of the Nile River and Africa's largest lake.

Toward a Better Tomorrow

In spite of its many problems, Africa does have several things in its favor. Its large population can be an advantage if more people receive a variety of educations. Many who complete high school work hard to get into Africa's colleges. If there isn't room, they apply to schools on other continents. Those who do not go to college or have little education are eager for work. Many learn new skills on the job. Some people, especially women, have started their own small businesses.

Africa also has a large percentage of some of the world's valuable natural resources—hardwood forests, rubber trees, oil, natural gas, gold, and diamonds. Careful use of these resources will provide jobs for many Africans, supply the money needed for better education

The future of Africa's rainforests depends on conservation and resource management.

and health care, and still protect the environment. Africa also has important sources of natural energy. East African countries use geothermal power as a source for electricity. This power comes from the heat generated by underground magma. Hydroelectric power is generated by dams on Africa's rivers. One dam that is being planned for the Congo River could produce enough electricity for the entire continent.

To better protect the environment, leaders in several African countries have started working together. One project is to build large parks and nature reserves that cross national boundaries. In that way, the animals that are being protected have plenty of room to roam in their natural habitats. Some leaders are also working to take better care of the rainforests. Individuals in the Sahel are planting trees and grasses to stop desertification. As Africans protect their environment, they will make life better for future generations.

Kgalagadi Transfrontier Park

Kgalagadi Transfrontier Park was Africa's first park that crossed national borders. In 2000, South Africa's Kalahari Gemsbok National Park was joined to Botswana's Gemsbok National Park. Sand dunes of the Kalahari Desert and thorn bushes, acacia trees, and grasses of the savanna cover this park. Small weaverbirds build huge nests in the trees. The kori bustard, which is the heaviest flying bird, is seen overhead. Gemsbok (oryx), springbok, and wildebeest migrate through the park. Those herds are thinned naturally by cheetahs, hyenas, leopards, and lions. This park protects many animals. It also provides jobs for guides, cooks, and housekeepers at the park's campsites.

GLOSSARY

chlorofluorocarbons chemicals used as coolants in refrigerators and air conditioners and as propellants in aerosol sprays

climate change an increase or decrease in temperature or rainfall over a long period of time

continent a large land mass

cyclone a storm with damaging winds and heavy rain that hits lands bordering the Indian Ocean

deforestation cutting down of entire forests

desertification weakening of soil from deforestation, drought, overuse of land, or climate change

drought a long period of time with little or no rainfall, making it hard to grow crops

endangered species a plant or animal that is in danger of becoming extinct

famine	a lack of food, often caused by drought, that can lead to thousands of deaths
habitat	the natural place in which a plant or animal lives
magma	hot, melted rock under Earth's surface; it flows from volcanoes as lava
open-pit mine	a large hole dug by miners and from which minerals are removed from the ground
plantation	a large farm where large amounts of one or two crops are grown
reservoir	the body of water, usually a lake, that forms behind a dam
rifting	the cracking and dropping of Earth's surface from tectonic plate movement
savanna	a flat, grassy plain with few or no trees in the tropics
tectonic plates	the hard sheets of moving rock that make up Earth's crust

FIND OUT MORE

BOOKS Aloian, Molly. *The Nile: River in the Sand*. Rivers Around the World. New York: Crabtree Publishing Company, 2010.

Pickford, Peter and Beverly Pickford. *African Safari: Into the Great Game Reserves*. Cape Town, South Africa: Africa Geographic, 2008.

Sandler, Michael. *Deserts: Surviving in the Sahara*. X-Treme Places. New York: Bearport Publishing, 2005.

Simpson, Judith. *Africa*. Investigate series. North Vancouver, British Columbia: Whitecap Books, Ltd., 2010.

Wojahn, Rebecca and Donald Wojahn. *A Savanna Food Chain: A Who-Eats-What Adventure in Africa*. Follow That Food Chain. Minneapolis: Lerner Publications, 2009.

Woods, Michael. *Seven Natural Wonders of Africa*. Seven Wonders. Minneapolis: Twenty-First Century, 2009.

DVDS   *The Great Rift: Africa's Greatest Story.* BBC Worldwide, 2010.

The Marvels of Madagascar: The Beauty of Nature. Narrated by
    Greg Grainger. Goldhil Entertainment, 2011.

Scenic Routes Around the World: Africa. Questar, 2011.

WEBSITES   **Africa**
http://www.pbs.org/wnet/africa/index.html
A great website with special pages on the regions of Africa, a quiz, photos,
background from the PBS series Africa, and a special set of pages called
Africa for Kids.

African Wildlife Foundation (AWF)
http://www.awf.org
Informative website with separate pages on individual animal species,
conservation projects, and ways people are improving the environment
and their own lives.

INDEX

Page numbers in **boldface** are illustrations.

chlorofluorocarbons, 22

climate change, 9, 21–23, 30, 38
    causes of, 21–22, 24, 37
    results of, 22–23, 30
    see also chlorofluorocarbons;
        drought; famine; magma
continent, 5, **5**, 7, 8, 10, 12, 14, 17, 19,
    26, 28, 32, 39, 40
    changing temperatures, 20
    continents and change, 9
cyclone, 25
    see also natural disasters

deforestation, 26–27, 31
desert, 30, 35–36, **35**, 38, 41
desertification, 19, **22**, 29, 40
    effects on plants and animals, 39
disease, 23–24, 38

drought, 22, 27, 29, 34

earthquake, 9, 25
endangered species, 24
Equator, **8**, 20, 25

famine, 22

Great Rift Valley, 12, **12**, 14–15

chlorofluorocarbons, 22

habitat, 8, 26, 30–31, 40
    results of desertification and
        flooding, 39

lake, 16–17, 19, 30–31, 35, **39**
    desertification, 19

magma, 21, 25, 40
maps

Physical Map of Africa, 13
Political Map of Africa, 6
Mapping Skills
    Getting the Lay of the Land, 16
    Where in the World is Africa, 7
mountains, 14, 20, **21**, 23

natural disasters, 25
    see also cyclone; earthquake;
      volcano

open-pit mine, 17

plantation, 27
plateau, 12, 14, 16
pollution, 22, 31
population, 8, 21, 32, 35–37, 39
    changes in, 32
    effect on the natural environment,
      9
    expected growth, 33
rainforest, 26–27, **27**, 28, 37, 40, **40**
    animals, 27
    deforestation, 26

endangered people, 35
reservoir, 19
rifting, 9, 12, **15**
    see also Great Rift Valley; tectonic
      plate movement
river, 11, 16–17, **19**, 23–24, 30–31,
    33, 36, 38, **39**, 40

savanna, 21, 29–30, **29**, 35, 41
    animals and people, 29
    damage to, 37

tectonic plates, 9
tectonic plate movement, 11
    see also rifting
temperature, 21
    changes in, 22
    effects of climate change, 38
    highest recorded, 20
    lowest recorded, 20

volcano, 10–11, 14, 25

Patricia K. Kummer has a B.A. in history from St. Catherine University in St. Paul, Minnesota, and an M.A. in history from Marquette University in Milwaukee, Wisconsin. She has written chapters for several world history and American history textbooks and has authored more than sixty books about countries, states, natural wonders, inventions, and other topics. Among her books are two on the African countries of Cameroon and Côte d'Ivoire. Books she has written for Cavendish Square include *Working Horses* in the Horses! series and the seven books in the Climates and Continents series.